CRAFT BREWS

the right glass for the right beer

ales and lagers
beer cocktails
food pairings with craft beers

by Robert Zollweg

Designed and written by Robert Zollweg
Photography by Rick Luettke, www.luettkestudio.com
Graphics by Gary Raschke and Robert Zollweg
Art Direction by Gary Raschke

Library of Congress Cataloging-in-Publication Data:

Craft Brews
The Right Glass for the Right Beer
by Robert Zollweg

www.zollwegart.com

ISBN 978-0-615-61530-1

Printed in the United States of America
By: R. R. Donnelley and Company

I'd like to dedicate this cookbook to

Dan Ibele

For his passion and understanding of the beer industry,
and a great friend and associate.

To my mother, Virginia, my kids, Christopher & Sandy and Rhonda & Doug
and all their children:
Kaylie, Andrew, Bret, Morgan and Korrin
To Steve Tester, Elaine and Tom Bender, Richard and Sandra Zollweg
Judy and Carl Sims, all their families
and to Annie.

There are so many people to thank for making this book a reality.

Gary Raschke, who has been there every step of the way. I could not have
made it happen without his help and knowledge.
My photographer, Rick Luettke and Bill Muzzillo's great literary skills.
Beth Baroncini, Karen Barentzen, Cathie Logan, Tom Fratantuono,
Denise Grigg, Kelly Kelley, Gina Baccari, Roger Williams, Jeff Joyce,
Serena Williams, Jessica Adler, Vicki Richardson, Amy Lewarchik, Greg Pax,
Brooks Clayton, Natalie Brunner, Sandy Shultz, Brionna Richmond,
Melissa Fleig, Fran Breitner, Ericka Sabo, Rosie Jordan,
Joe Mefferd, Brenda Bennett and Pete Kasper.

Jerry Moore, Dennis Gage, Susan Asp, Bobby DeSeyn and Eli Markho
for all their help in researching this project.

and to Libbey Glass
for giving me the opportunity to do what I enjoy doing.

5

Table of Contents

Introduction

Craft Brews is a simple book that will try to explain the various ways to learn and understand what Craft Beer is all about.

I have divided this book into various chapters. Each one will explain a different aspect of what is needed to know about Craft Beer. You'll find a brief history on how to serve it, what to serve it in, what to serve it with, some beer cocktail recipes and other fun ways to use Craft Beers.

My ideas behind **Craft Brews** started when I noticed all the different specialty beers in various liquor and beverage stores. There used to be just a few shelves from the big name breweries. But today, most beverage stores have a whole section or department with craft beers from all over the country as well as the world.

Craft Brews tasting and food pairing is what the wine industry has been doing for years, telling all of us that we need to serve the wine with certain foods and at certain temperatures and in the proper glass. Craft Brews and specialty beers are right up there with their sister, the wine industry when it come to serving this or any beverage properly.

Restaurants have been seeing an increase in popularity with serving Craft Beers. They are not just another standard everyday beer. They demand a higher selling price and a proper glass in which to serve these special beers. As a result, the glass industry has started developing new and exciting glass shapes. Restaurants are serving these specialty beers in a proper glass to enhance the qualities of the beer. To make them special and more exciting, they have found ways to showcase these beers with special menus, beer and food pairings and beer tastings.

Craft Brews are great for tasting parties. Invite your guests over for whatever occasion you are planning and serve wonderful appetizers and craft beers in mini beer glasses. There are many beer tasting glasses available in the marketplace today. These mini beer glasses are usually about 3-5 ounces each and are perfect for serving tasting samples of various craft beers to your guests. I felt this was something today's consumer would love and were missing in the marketplace, especially when it comes to home entertaining. **Craft Brews** is the new wine.

Over the next few pages I will explain what Craft Brews is all about, from the proper glassware to the proper food to serve with it.

I am by no means an expert on beer, but I do know how to entertain. Entertaining with Craft Brews is a wonderful new experience for all of us to enjoy today.

Working in the tabletop industry has been very rewarding and it is where I have learned so much about entertaining. I love to entertain and I hope that **Craft Brews** will be a great way for you to turn your next festive occasion, cocktail or tasting party into something really special.

Enjoy !   Robert

History of Craft Beer

The History of Craft Beers

Beer in general has been said to have been around for over 5,000 years and is the oldest known beverage in the world today, excluding water. Some say beer and wine were developed at the same time. Wine was considered luxurious for royalty and the upper-class, while beer was for the commoners. A few of the oldest breweries in the world still operating are: the Weihenstephan Brewery in Freising, Bavaria, the Weltenburg Abbey Brewery and the Zatec Brewery in the Czech Republic, all dating back to around 1000-1050 AD.

Craft Beers and the Craft Breweries got their first start in the early 1960's. They were originally called Microbreweries, but today they are known as craft breweries. The American Northwest, notably Portland, Oregon is known as the birthplace of craft brewing. Probably the first person who saw the vision and need for high quality beers in America was Fritz Maytag, the washing machine founder. Fritz purchased the struggling Anchor Steam Brewing Company in San Francisco and turned it into a craft brew powerhouse. That was the beginning of the craft beer industry in the United States.

A few breweries failed and a few made in through these beginning times, but ultimately the microbrew concept took off, inspiring numerous others to brew hand crafted unique beers with high quality ingredients and changing the way Americans felt about beer. Since then there have been hundreds of small craft breweries in almost every state in the country.

A Brewpubs was the original name for a small brewery that produced and served its beer on site. If more than 75% of its beer is distributed off site then it is a microbrewery. Craft breweries are small, locally owned breweries. Macro or Megabreweries are the big giants of the beer world. The largest mega brewery in the world is the Belgium-American company of Anheuser-Busch InBev.

The brewing process is usually divided into nine steps: malting, milling, mashing, lautering, boiling, fermenting, conditioning, filtering and filling (packaging). The basic ingredients of beer are: hops, grain, malt, yeast and water, with water being 95%. Early breweries used copper kettles or vats in the brewhouse, but after the Industrial Revolution, almost all breweries now use stainless steel equipment.

Great beer should have taste and it's their flavor that make them great. A really great beer begins with aroma, then comes into the texture and flavor and ends with the finish. Really great beers have a long and lingering finish.

It has been said by many true Cicerone's, that America has only recently come into great beers. The mass produced beer typically purchased from a grocery store or carry out is just an alcoholic beverage and really does not resemble a truly great beer.

Some might agree or disagree, but once you start to experience some of the new craft beers of today, you will better understand what is a truly great beer.

I need to mention the grandfather of all beer knowledge and that is the late Michael Jackson. Michael devoted his whole life to understanding and sharing his knowledge of craft beers and was one of the first to say "you need to drink the right beer from the right glass"
Michael has written many books on beer and if you are really interested in knowing everything about beer, read his famous book "The Great Beer Guide."

What is a Brewmaster ?

A brewmaster is the person who is in charge of the production of the beer and is someone who has mastered the art of brewing beer.

Jon Koester, Brewmaster at the Maumee Bay Brewing Company in Toledo took a few minutes to explain to me all the ins and outs of his daily duties as head brewmaster.

The overall fermentation process for ales is typically 2 weeks or more and for lagers about 4 weeks. The main ingredients in craft beer are malted barley, hops, water and yeast. Maumee Bay brews both ales and lagers. We do all sorts of fruit or spiced specialty beers. Some of the styles that they have done are: Dark Chocolate Cheery Porter, King Prunus Apricot Wheat, Strawberry Kolsch, Summer Stinger and Blitzen Ale.

Craft beers have had their ups and downs over the past 20 years or so, but it is apparent that it is going nowhere but up lately with the diversity of types of beers and sales are constantly growing.

One of Jon's most rewarding moments is when he goes into the brew pub or any bar that serves his beer and meets the people who have a passion for craft beers and are enjoying his beer.

Jon told me everyone in the craft beer industry is so creative, helpful and supportive. If he ever needed any advice on something, he won't hesitate to ask any fellow brewer because they are all so willing to help. He said it's a great time to be in the beer industry and to be part of the craft beer revolution. So Cheers !

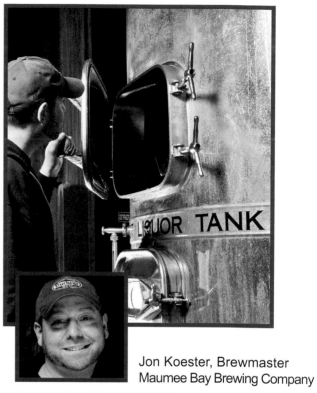

Jon Koester, Brewmaster
Maumee Bay Brewing Company

Photos taken at the Maumee Bay Brewing Company, Toledo, Ohio by Brooks Clayton

SOMMOLIER vs. CICERONE™

A Wine Sommolier is an expert wine steward. One who has the knowledge and understanding of all types of wines, on serving wine, decanting the wine, suggesting the right wine with the right food. There is no real certification when it comes to being a wine sommolier, but all good restaurants with an established wine list will normally have a wine sommolier.

A Beer Sommolier is a person who understands proper storage and serving of beer, with expertise in selecting, acquiring and serving this beer, but without certification.

There is another new term that describes a connoisseur of beer, Cicerone. The term Cicerone is to beer as Sommolier is to wine.

A Cicerone is a person with expertise in beer and who can guide consumers to enjoyable and high-quality experiences with great beer. That person will also know all about proper storage and serving temperatures of craft beers.

But a Certified Cicerone or a Master Cicerone is the ones who has passed the requisite test of knowledge and tasting skills to get the certification from the National Brewers Association and the Craft Beer Institute.

This certification is called the Cicerone Certification Program. This program is run by Ray Daniels, president of the Craft Beer Institute and serves as a testing and certification authority for all beer servers, consultants and others in the craft beer and brewing trade. To find out more about the Cicerone Certification Program go to www.cicerone.org.

Various Craft Beers in the Marketplace

What are the various types of Craft Beers ?

On the following pages I will describe to you some of the most popular craft beers in the marketplace today. But believe me, before I finish writing this book there will be many more available in the states and worldwide. Craft Beers have taken the beer industry by storm in the past few years. They are cool and trendy and equally as delicious.

I'd be remiss if I said I could show you all the various craft brews that are available today. I've selected the ones that are more national or that I feel are a little more unique and different. But there are many, many more to choose from and many of them are outstanding. I always stay away from the big breweries that claim their beers are craft beers. Look for the small local ones with fantastic graphics on their beer cartons.

There are two major types of beer brewed today, one is ale and the other is lager. Both are considered beer. There are a few specialty beers that do not fit into either of these two categories. They are Fruit, Spiced and Smoked Beers, Mead Beers, Ciders, California Common or Steam Beer, Kolsch and Altbiers. I will explain some of the general characteristics about each.

I want to take a minute and describe what the average American thinks about beer. They usually think that all good beer is brewed by the big guys: Anheuser-Busch InBev, Miller Brewing Company, Coors, etc. They have come to think that this is good beer while most Europeans think these beers are just a cold alcoholic beverage to say the least.

The big guys have done a great job for years in providing the average adult with a cold alcoholic beverage. But things are changing, some of these adults are looking for new and exciting beers with all sorts of unique and different flavors. Thus the craft beer industry was born and is now flourishing beyond our wildest imaginations.

Storing Beer: Always store beer in a carton in a cool, dry place, away from light and heat. Refrigerators are ok for some beers, but not vintage ones. The basement or cellar is an ideal location for storing beer.

ALES

Ales are generally fruity, complex and heavier tasting beers that are best when served cool, about 50-60 degrees F. They are made with top-fermenting yeasts that rise to the surface when fermenting, which occurs at warmer temperatures in just a matter of days in the brewing process.

Abbey Dubbel - Trappist
English Bitter, Best, ESB Ales
Stouts and Russian Imperial Stouts
Abbey Tripel-Trappist
Strong Golden Ales
Scottish & Strong Scottish Ales
American Wheats
India Pale Ale, IPA & Imperial IPA
English Old & Strong Old Ales
Red Ales (Amber)
Lambics
Saison & Farmhouse Ales
Brown Ale
Pale Ale
Wheat, Weissbiers & Hefe-Weisen
Barley Wine
White Ale - Witbier
Weizenbock-Maibock
Porter
Blonde & Cream Ale

LAGERS

Lager beers, from the German word "to store," are made from bottom fermenting yeasts that ferment at the bottom of liquids at colder temperatures over a longer period of time than ales, usually four or more weeks. Lagers are usually clear, crisp and cleaner tasting than that of ales and best when served colder at 39-46 degrees F (4-8C)

The pilsner style lager, famous for its very light and clean taste, was first brewed in Pilsen, Bohemia in 1842. It was made famous by the original Urquell Pilsner brand.

American Amber Lager
Dark Bock
Oktoberfest - Marzen
Dark Lager
Munich Dunkel Lager
Bock-Doppelbock
Helles
Maibock-Weizenbock
Classic Pilsners
Standard American Lager
Pale Bock, Heller Bock, Maibock
Premium Lager - Pale Lager
Dortmunder -Dunkel

OTHER SPECIALTY BEERS

Specialty beers are made from ales or lagers or a combination of both. Some are infused with fruits and spices or brewed with a unique twist that will dramatically change the flavor and aromas. Smoked beers are made with a unique flavor and aroma from malt that has been dried over wood smoke. Fruit and spiced beers are derived from adding fruit and or spices during the fermenting process that take on a more unusual flavor similar to wines. Steam beers are made with lager yeasts but brewed at ale temperatures. They use coolships to cool the beer. Steam rises from the cooling beer and that gives it the name Steam Beer.

California Common Beer &
Anchor Steam Beer

Kolsch & Altbiers
Cream & Blonde Ales
Hyper Beers

Chili Beer
Pumpkin Beer
Spiced Beer
Honey Beer
Smoked Beer
Fruit Beer
Hybrid Beer

Styles
of
Glassware

The Proper Glassware for Craft Beers

The following pages will show you some wonderful glass items for serving craft and specialty beers. There are many more different styles of glassware in the marketplace that will work for serving beer as well. I'll try to show you a few that really compliment the beer and that are readily available in today's retail stores.

Brewmasters in the states are getting more particular about what glass to serve their beer in than ever before. Europeans have been doing it for years. In the next chapter I will show a particular style of beer and the proper glass to serve that beer in. This is according to various resources, on line information and interviews I have completed in the past few months from all my new friends at the local beer store.

Glassware should always be sparkling clear and clean, free of soap suds and any oily residue that will destroy the head, flavor and aroma of any good beer.

Here's a collection of various beer pilsners that are perfect for serving classic European Pilsners and other Pale Lagers. Pilsner glasses showcase a beer's color, clarity and carbonation. The conical shape helps maintain the beer's head, while the narrow design allows the aromas to reach your nose, providing the ultimate beer experience.

Here is a great collection of pub style glasses that offers the perfect presentation of Classic Ales such as English and Irish Porters, IPA's, Pale Ales, Brown Ales or Stouts. They feature a wide mouth to support the frothy head and will offer a brilliant and traditional beer presentation.

These beautifully shaped bowls are ideal for Belgian Ales, American Lagers, Brown Ales, Saison and some Lambics and are well suited for specialty fruit and spiced beers.

These tall beer glasses are ideal for serving Wheat beer or Weissen beers, Weizenbocks, Pale Lagers, Dortmunders and standard American Lagers. The wide or rounded tops are designed to hold a generous head of foam, which is ideal for holding in the carbonation that accentuates the flavors and aromas.

This classic thistle glass is perfect for Scottish Ales.

Great looking beer mugs and steins for Doppelbock and Dortmunder German Lagers, Oktoberfests and Dunkels.

These are the perfect glasses with rounded and chalice style bowls for serving Abbey Dubells, Abbey Tripel and all Trappist Ales, they are also ideal for Barley Wines and some Strong Golden Ales.

These unique shapes are reminiscent of traditional brandy glasses but are ideal for serving any dark robust beers, like Russian Imperial Stouts, Abbey Dubbels and Abbey Tripels, Strong Golden Ales, Doppelbocks, Barley Wines, Spiced Beers and all Hyper Beers.

The Right Glass for Each Style of Craft Beer

Abbey Dubbel (Trappists)

Part of the Trappist or Abbey family of Belgium brewed ales. A slightly strong reddish brown ale, whose body is thinned by the use of sugar in the recipe.

Some of the characteristics of Abbey Dubbel ales are: they are a strong, lightly hopped, deep amber ale with a dry to modest body. They have complex caramel, raisin and fruity flavors with a crisp finish.

Average alcohol by volume is: 6.0 - 7.8 %

Abbey Dubbel Ales are best when served at 50 - 55 degrees F.

Some ideal food pairings would be barbecue, meat stews, grilled steaks and smoked rib roast. Also, Abbey type of cheeses and French Morbier, milk chocolate desserts, chocolate bread pudding and butter truffles.

Some of the top selling Abbey Dubbels in North America are:

Affligem Dubbel   Westmalle Dubbel
Chimay Premiere Red   Lost Abbey, Lost and Found
Ommegang Abbey Ale   Allegash Dubbel Reserve

The ideal glass shapes for serving Abbey Dubbel are shown on the next page.

Abbey Tripel (Trappists) & Strong Golden Ales

A strong and sophisticated group of beers with Trappist origins, such as Abbey Tripel, Golden Strong and Dark Strong Ales are all part of this family of Strong Ales.

Trappist ales are only brewed by the Belgian monks in Belgium. When this ale is produced elsewhere in the world, it is known as an Abbey Ale. There are seven monasteries that brew Trappist Ales. They are: Chimay, Westmalle, Orval, Westvleteren, La Trappe, Achel and Rochefort.

Some of the unique characteristics of Trappist-Abbey Ales and Strong Golden Ales are: they are fruity, spicey and strong with complex flavors and earthy, hoppy aromas. They are also moderately hopped with sugar added for drinkability, smooth and light-bodied and honey colored with a creamy head of foam.

Average alcohol by volume is: 7.5 - 9.5%.

Trappist-Abbey Ales and Strong Golden Ales are best when served at 40 - 45 degrees F.

Some ideal food pairings would be spicy Cajun food, crab cakes, pheasant and roasted turkey. Also any non-chocolate dessert like apricot amaretto tart and baklava.

Some of the top selling brands of Strong Golden Ales, Abbey Tripel or Trappist Ales in North America are:

Belgian Duval
La Trappe Dubbel
Chimay CinQ Cents White
Unibroue La Fin du Monde
Orval

Chimay Grande Reserve
Westmalle Trappist Tripel
Westvleteren 8
Rochefort 10

The ideal glass shapes for a Strong Golden Ale, Abbey or Trappist Ale are shown on the next page. It is always served in a chalice-styled stem.

Red Ale (Amber)

Some of the unique characteristics of Red Ales are: they are sweet, medium-bodied, reddish amber ales with burnt sugar to caramel malt flavors and light to medium hop bitterness. This is a moderate strength ale, not based on any particular style.

Average alcohol by volume is: 4.0 - 6.0%.

Red Ales are best when served at 50 - 55 degrees F.

Some ideal food pairings would be from a wide range of foods, like grilled chicken, seafood, burgers, spicy cuisine. Great with light tangy cheeses and desserts like poached pears, banana pound cake and pecan lace cookies.

Some of the top selling brands of Red Ales in North America are:

Alaskan Amber
Anderson Valley Boont Amber Ale
Magic Hat Humble Patience
Murphy's Irish Amber
Pete's Wicked Red Rush
Smithwick's Amber Ale

Flat Tire Amber Ale
Bear Republic Red Rocket
Full Sail Amber
New Belgium Flat Tire
Domaine DuPage Amber Ale
Killian's Irish Red

The ideal glass shapes for a Red Ale are shown on the next page.

American Wheat

Originating in the Pacific Northwest, these hazy, wheat ales are fermented with normal ale yeast. They are very light in color with a creamy texture. Some of the additional characteristics of American Wheat Ales are: they are crisp and refreshing, with light to moderate hopping. The wheat adds a soft, creamy texture and sometimes fruit is added for unique variations.

Average alcohol by volume is 3.5 - 5.5 %.

American Wheat Ales are best when served at 40 - 45 degrees F.

Some ideal food pairings with American Wheat Ales are: very light, crispy salads, vegetable dishes, chicken and sushi. Buffalo Mozzarella and Wisconsin brick cheeses work well also. Not something that works well with desserts, but fresh berries or thin wafer type cookies are ok.

Some of the top selling brands of American Wheat Ales in North America are:

Boulevard Unfiltered Wheat
Goose Island 312 Urban Wheat
Leinenkugal Honey Wheat
Three Floyd's Gumballhead Wheat Ale
Widmer Hefeweizen

The ideal glass shapes for American Wheat Ale are shown on the next page.

Barley Wine Ales

English in origin, some of the unique characteristics of Barley Wine Ales are that they are more closely related to fine ports and sherries. They are a strong, rich and lightly carbonated ale with a fruity malt sweetness and a very strong alcohol presence. They are copper to mahogany in color and are best served as an aperitif or nightcap that can be sipped.

Average alcohol by volume is: 8.0 - 12.0%.

Barley Wine Ales are best when served at 50 - 55 degrees F.

Some ideal food pairings would be fresh, gamey meats, strong cheeses and dark, rich desserts like a chocolate hazelnut torte or a toffee caramel cheesecake. This ale will easily overpower most main dishes.

Some of the top selling brands of Barley Wine Ales in North America are:

Anchor Old Foghorn
Dogfish Head Olde School
Rogue Old Crustacean
Sierra Nevada Bigfoot
Victory Old Horizontal
John Barleycorn Barleywine Ale

Cucada Barleywine Ale
O'Hanlon's Thomas Hardy's Ale
J. W. Lee's Harvest Ale
Bridgeport Brewing Old Knucklehead
Hog Heaven Barleywine Ale
Ale Smith Old Numbskull

The ideal glass shapes for a Barley Wine Ale are shown on the next page.

English Bitter, Best or ESB Bitter Ales

Originally brewed in England, Bitter is an English term for Pale Ale. Some of the unique characteristics of Bitter Ales are: they are light bodied, distinctively bitter, with fresh hops plus nutty maltiness and a crisp finish. The hops intensity ranges from ordinary bitter to extra special bitter or ESB.

Average alcohol by volume Ordinary Bitter is 2.4 - 3 %, for Best Bitter 3.3 - 3.8 %, for ESB Bitter 4.8 - 5 %.

Bitter Ales are best when served at 50 - 55 degrees F.

Some ideal food pairings would be fish and chips, roasted chicken or pork, mild cheeses and rich meats. Oatmeal raisin walnut cookies are a great compliment for something sweet to accompany this ale.

Some of the top selling brands of Bitter Ales in the North America are:

Fuller's ESB
Gritty's Best Bitter
Redhook ESB
Rogue Younger's Special Bitter
Pyramid Alehouse ESB

Goose Island Honker's Ale
Anchor Small Beer
Ridgeway Ivanhoe
Coniston Bluebird Bitter Ale

The ideal glass shapes for a Bitter Ale are shown on the next page.

A gift from
Gabrielle Sauer

Happy Birthday!! Here is something to enhance your beer snobbery and impress others in your new, classy life. Also, you'll be happy to know I bought it from Amazon. Love always, Gabrielle

Brown Ale

Originally from England, some of the unique characteristics of Brown Ales are: they are dark and well-balanced with light nutty maltiness, roasted malty flavors, hop bitterness and a clean crisp finish. Amber to brown in color.

Average alcohol by volume is: 4.0 - 6.0%.

Brown Ales are best when served at 50 - 55 degrees F.

Some ideal food pairings would be grilled salmon, roasted pork, smoked sausage and Gouda cheese. For desserts a pecan maple walnut cake, pear fritters or cashew brittle.

Some of the top selling brands of Brown Ales in North America are:

Brooklyn Brown Ale	Goose Island Hex Nut Brown Ale
Newcastle Brown Ale	Dogfish Head Indian Brown Ale
Pete's Wicked Ale	Surley Beender
Samuel Smith's Nut Brown Ale	Moose Drool Brown Ale

The ideal glass shapes for a Brown Ale are shown on the next page.

Imperial Stout

The Imperial Stout is sometimes refered to as the Russian Imperial Stout. These black and brown ales from ancient England that have diminished in recent years but have become more important in Ireland.

Some characteristics of Imperial Stout are: they are a high gravity black beer, massively roasty, often with considerable hopping. It is a very intense, sipping style of beer.

Average alcohol by volume is 7.0 - 12.0 %.

Imperial Stouts should be served at 50 - 55 degrees F.

Imperial Stout easily overpowers most foods, but some foods that will stand up to this strong ale are smoked goose and grilled steaks with a heavy sauce. Gouda, Parmesan, Sharp cheddar and aged cheeses will work well with an Imperial Stout, as do rich desserts like dark chocolate truffles, chocolate raspberry mousse cake or black forest torte.

Some of the top selling Imperial Stouts in North America are:

Courage Imperial Stout
Stone Imperial Stout
North Coast Old Rasputin Imperial
Harvey's Le Coq Imperial Extra Stout

Russian Imperial Stout
Three Floyds Dark Load
Stout Bell's Expedition Stout
Bear Republic Big Bear Black Stout

The ideal glass shapes for serving Imperial Stout are shown on the next page.

IPA: India Pale Ale & Imperial IPA

This ale was originally developed as an export beer to export from England to India, thus the name. Some of the unique characteristics of IPA's are: it has a strong, dry and medium bodied flavor with a good malt balance. The style IPA has intense or strong hop bitterness, flowery aromas and medium maltiness, with a dry, crisp finish.

The words Imperial and IPA, has been used for more than a century to designate a strong, luxurious bitter beer and twice as strong as a regular IPA. Double IPA means it is extra strong or double the alcoholic content. Imperials are usually used for special occasions.

Average alcohol by volume for IPA is: 4.5 - 7.5%, Imperial IPA is 7.5 - 10.5 %.

India Pale Ales are best when served at 50 - 55 degrees F.

Some ideal food pairings would be strong, spicy foods with curry, grilled lamb and milder blue cheeses like Gorgonzola or Cambozola. Sweet desserts would be carrot cake, caramel apple tart, ginger spice cake, creme brulee and persimmon rice pudding.

Some of the top selling brands of IPA's and Imperials IPA's in North America are:

Dogfish Head 60 Minute IPA	Goose Island IPA
Founders Centennial IPA	Wild Goose IPA
Ballast Point Sculpin IPA	Harpoon IPA
Sierra Nevada Celebration Ale	Dogfish Head 90 Minute Imperial IPA
Bear Republic Racer 5	Stone Ruination Imperial IPA
Shipyard IPA	Russian River Pliny the Elder Imperial IPA
Bell's Two Hearted IPA	Rogue Imperial IPA

The ideal glass shapes for a IPA or Imperial IPA are shown on the next page.

Lambics

Lambics are an ancient family of sour beers, originally brewed in the region of Belgium, near Brussels, at the Cantillon Brewery. They are fermented with wild yeasts and bacteria and originally made from pale ales, often hazy with an aromatic blend of fruity and earthy flavors with almost no hop bitterness or aroma. Always intensely dry and fruity with complex earthy and cider-like flavors. Lambics are low in carbonation, winy tasting and honey amber in color and very refreshing. Some refer to it as the champagne of beer.

Average alcohol by volume is: 5.0 - 7.0 %.

Lambic are best when served at 40 - 45 degrees F.

Some ideal food pairings would be light seafood dishes, pates, steamed mussels, sweet and herb cheeses, chocolates and chocolaty desserts along with panna cotta with lemon.

Some of the top selling brands of Lambic Ales in North America are:

Lindeman's Framboise   Boon Gueuze Mariage Parfait
Cantillon Rose de Gambrinus   Oud Beersel Lambic
Hanssens Artisanal Oude Kriek   St. Sylvestre 3 Monts
Dogfish Head Festiva Lente
New Belgium La Folie

Cantillon Grand Cru Bruocsella, considered by most to be the most expensive beer in the world, sells somewhere around $800.00 USD per bottle.

The ideal glass shapes for a Lambic are shown on the next page.

Pale Ales (English & American)

Pale Ales are a family of golden to amber flavored ales. Some of the unique characteristics of Pale Ales are: dry and hoppy with some fruitiness on top of malt that is sometimes bready or nutty and medium-bodied with good malt balance. Pale Ales are golden to copper in color.

Average alcohol by volume is: 3.8 - 6.2%.

Pale Ales are best when served at 50 - 55 degrees F.

With a wide range of food pairings, some ideal food pairings would be meat pies, burgers, English cheeses such as cheddar or Derby with sage. Some ideal desserts would be pumpkin flan, maple bread pudding and bananas foster.

Some of the top selling brands of Pale Ales in North America are:

Bass Ale
Samuel Smith's Old Brewery Pale Ale
Tetley's English Ale
Morland's Old Speckled Hen
Anchor Liberty Ale Cisco
Sierra Nevada Pale Ale
Cucap Chupacabras Pale Ale

Whitbread Pale Ale
Odell 5 Barrel Pale Ale
North Coast Ruedrich's Red Seal
Boulder Brewing Hazed & Infused
Hooker American Pale Ale
Whale's Tale Pale Ale
De Rank XXX Bitter

The ideal glass shapes for a Pale Ale are shown on the next page.

Porters

Porters are the original black beer of England. The unique characteristics of Porters are: dark and bitter with light bodied hoppiness flavors, along with soft roasted coffee and sometimes chocolate flavors. They are slightly paler than a Stout.

Average alcohol by volume is: 4.5 - 6.5%.

Porters are best when served at 50 - 55 degrees F.

Some ideal food pairings would be roasted or smoked food, barbecue, sausages, roasted red meats and blackened fish. Ideally suited for Gruyere cow milk cheeses and chocolate peanut butter cookies, toasted coconut cookies and various chocolate desserts.

Some of the top selling brands of Porters in North America are:

Fuller's London Porter
Samuel Smith's Taddy Porter
Smuttynose Robust Porter
Yakima Grant's Perfect Porter
Pripps Carnegie Porter

Flag Porter
Great Lakes Edward Fitzgerald Porter
Full Sail Top Sail American Porter
Flying Dog Gonzo Imperial Porter

The ideal glass shapes for a Porter are shown on the next page.

White Ale or Witbier

This is a soft, hazy style of golden pale ale, said to have originated from farmhouse breweries of Northwest Belgium. Some of the unique characteristics of these Belgium White Ales are: They have dry, crisp, complex flavors of fruits and spices, with earthy floral aromas and bitterness. They are sometimes flavored with star anise and dried orange peels. It is incredibly refreshing, tart and medium bodied with a bubbly white head.

Average alcohol by volume is: 4.5 - 8.1%.

White Ales are best when served at 40 - 45 degrees F.

Some ideal food pairings would be lighter seafood dishes and steamed mussels and clams, Mascarpone and herb cheese spreads on crackers. Ideal desserts would be banana orange crepes, orange sorbet and panna cotta with lemon.

Some of the top selling brands of White Ales in North America are:

Blue Moon White Beer
Hoegarden Original White Ale
Bell's Winter White Ale
Michigan Brewing Company Celis White
Fantome
Hoegaard Original White

Stevens Point Belgium White
Key West Southern Most White
Pike Place Dry White
Mothership Wit
Sweetwater Hummer
Allagash White

The ideal glass shapes for White Ale are shown on the next page.

Scottish & Strong Scotch Ales

This strong mahogany colored beer is a unique Scottish specialty. Some of the characteristics of Scottish Ales are: dark, malty and sweet tastes, ranging in body and strength from light to slightly heavy. The contain a rich maltiness with sweet toffee, butterscotch flavors and are dark brown in color.

Average alcohol by volume is: 2.8 - 10.0 %.

Scottish Ales are best when served at 50 - 55 degrees F.

Some ideal food pairings would be roasted or grilled lamb, beef, various game and smoked salmon. This beer is especially good when served with sticky toffee puddings and chocolate chip shortbreads, as well as aged sheep cheese.

Some of the top selling brands of Scottish Ales in North America are:

Belhaven 801
Caledonian MacAndrew's Scotch Ale
Grant's Scottish Ale
McEwan's Scotch Ale
Caledonian 701
Orkney Skull Footer

Samuel Adams Scotch Ale
Odell's 90 Shilling
Red Hill Scotch Ale
Traquair House Ale
Belhaven Wee Heavy
Ale Smith Wee Heavy

The ideal glass shapes for a Scotch Ale are shown on the next page.

Stouts

Stouts are black beers with a number of substyles, including dry irish stout, sweet london stout and creamy oatmeal stout. Stouts are from the ale family. Originally from Ireland and England, some of the unique characteristics of Stouts are: very dark brown to black in color, bitter and roasted malt always dominating the nose. Serve with medium roasted coffee and burnt chocolate flavors that are sweet, creamy, dry and bitter.

Average alcohol by volume is: 3.0 - 12.0%.

Stouts are best when served at 50 - 55 degrees F.

Some ideal food pairings would be hearty rich foods, such as steaks, meat pies, raw oysters, scallops and other shellfish. Great with Irish Cheddar cheeses and a chocolate souffle, tiramisu and mocha mascarpone mousse for desserts.

Some of the top selling brands of Stouts in North America are:

Guinness Stout Draught
Anderson Valley Barney Flats Oatmeal Stout
Three Floyd's Black Sun Stout
North Coast Old Rasputin Russian Stout
Murphy's Stout

Beamish Stout
Rogue Shakespeare Stout
Victory Storm King Stout
North Coast Old 38
Goose Island Dublin Stout

The ideal glass shapes for a Stout are shown on the next page.

English Old & Strong Ale

This is a loose group of strong amber to brown ales. Old Ales have been aged in wood and then blended with strong ale. Some of the unique characteristics of English Old & Strong Ales are: strong, dark and full-bodied, with rich fruit flavors of currants, caramel, burnt coffee, molasses, chocolate and malt flavors. They also have additional hints of toast, leather and wood. Like a rare cognac or fine sherry, many strong ales improve with age.

Average alcohol by volume is: 6.0 - 11.0%.

English Old & Strong Ales are best when served at 50 - 55 degrees F.

Some ideal food pairings would be big, intense dishes such as roast beef, lamb or wild game, grilled or roasted. Rich and moderately aged cheeses and spiced plum-walnut crisp, classic canolli and toffee apple crisp.

Some of the top selling brands of English Old & Strong Ales in North America are:

Theakston's Old Peculiar
Thomas Hardy's Ale
Fuller's Vintage Ale
Gale's Prize Old Ale
J.W.Lees Harvest Ale

North Coast Old Stock Ale
Pyramid Snow Cap Ale
Greene King Olde Suffolk Ale
Stone Arrogant Bastard

The ideal glass shapes for a English Old & Strong Ale are shown on the next page.

Wheat, Weissbier, Hefe-weisen Beers

Weiss means wheat and Hefe means yeast, so wheat beers are made from wheat and yeast. Some of the unique characteristics of Wheat Beers are: crisp and light-bodied with a slight citrus tang, a dry palate and a very creamy texture. They are usually a little cloudy in color or appearance.

Average alcohol by volume is: 2.5 - 9.3%.

Wheat Beers are best when served at 40 - 45 degrees F.

Some ideal food pairings would be lighter foods, such as salads, seafood and sushi. Ideal for mid morning brunch. Also good with simple goat cheeses and strawberry shortcakes, fruit trifle, key lime pie and other light desserts.

Some of the top selling brands of Wheat Beers in North America are:

Goose Island 312 Urban Wheat	Aventinus
Leinenkugal's Honey Wheat	Bell's Oberon
Paulaner Hefe-Weizen	American Wheat
Kindl Berliner Weisse	Erdinger Weissbier
Schneider Weisse Weizenhell	Weihenstephaner Hefe Weissbier

The ideal glass shapes for a Wheat Beer are shown on the next page.

Saison-Farmhouse Ales

The Saison style of ale originated in the farmhouses of Wallonia, Belgium and is sometimes called Country Beer or Farmhouse Ale. Saison is the French word for season. This ale is brewed in the winter and drunk in the summer. Some of the characteristics of Saison Ales are: dry and crisp with complex flavors of fruit, spices and floral aromas and a slight tartness or bitterness, with a refreshing crispness and dry finish. They are sometimes hazy and golden in color.

Average alcohol by volume is: 5.0 - 8.0 %.

Saisons are best when served at 40 - 45 degrees F.

Some ideal food pairings would be: lighter seafood dishes, herb flavored cheeses and fruity desserts like banana orange crepes, sorbets and light lemon chiffons.

Some of the top selling brands of Saison Ales in North America are:

Saison Dupont
Le Merle Saison
Hennepin Farmhouse Saison
Saison De Lente
Saison Fantone

Jolly Pumpkin Bam Biere
Lost Abbey Red Barn Ale
Boulevard Saison
Southampton Saison Deluxe

The ideal glass shapes for a Saison Ale are shown on the next page.

American Amber Lagers & Oktoberfest

Oktoberfest, American Amber Lager, Vienna Lager and Marzen are all part of the Amber Lager family with the emphasis on malt. Some of the unique characteristics of Amber Lagers are: clean, with a modest caramel taste and mildly sweet with roasted malt flavors and low hop presence.

Oktoberfest Lagers are made in breweries only in Munich, Germany. Vienna Lager is brewed in Austria and Marzen Lager is from Bavaria.

Average alcohol by volume is: 3.5 - 6.0%.

Amber Lagers are best when served at 45 - 50 degrees F.

Some ideal food pairings would be hearty spicy foods, Mexican foods, barbecue, chili con carne, sausage and pork. It is the perfect beer for spicy jalapeno jack cheese, white cheddar and brick cheese. Some ideal desserts would be mango or coconut flan, spice cakes, passion fruit bread pudding and almond biscotti.

Some of the top selling brands of Amber Lagers in North America are:

Aylinger Oktoberfest Marzen	Stoudt's Oktoberfest
Paulaner Oktoberfest Marzen	August Schell Firebrick Amber Lager
Spaten Oktoberfest Ur Marzen	Samuel Adams Oktoberfest
Thomas Hooker Oktoberfest	Widmer Oktoberfest
Summit Oktoberfest	Goose Island Oktoberfest

The ideal glass shapes for a Amber Lager are shown on the next page.

Dark Bock & Doppelbock Beer (Lager)

The Bock Family of strong lagers was originally conceived to skirt around the fasting rules of Lent. Bocks are always strong and malty and the stronger ones are often fairly sweet. Some of the unique characteristics of Bock Lagers are: strong and full-bodied with a smooth, malty aroma and flavor.

Average alcohol by volume is: 6.5 - 14.4%.

Bock Lagers are best when served at 45 - 50 degrees F.

Some ideal food pairings would be rich, roasted foods like duck or roasted pork shanks. Ideal with the classic Limberger cheese. Some great desserts would be German chocolate cake, Black Forest cake and dried fruit & rum tarts.

Some of the top selling brands of Bock Lagers in North America are:

Aass Bock	Anchor Bock Beer
Ayinger Celebrator Doppelbock	Stegmaier Brewhouse Bock Beer
Einbecker Mai-Ur-Bock	Leinenkugal's Big Butt Doppelbock
Samuel Adams Triple Bock	Tommyknocker Butthead Dopplebock
Schneider Aventinus Weizen Eisbock	Blonde Dopplebock Lager
Shiner Bock	Bell's Consecrator

The ideal glass shapes for a Bock Lager are shown on the next page.

Dark Lager & Dunkel Lager

Dark American Lagers, Munich Dunkel and Schwarzbier Lagers are a small family of malty beers with a varying caramel, toasty and subtle hopping of flavors. Some of the unique characteristics of Dark Lagers are: dark and well-balanced with roasted malty flavors, hop bitterness and a clean dry finish.

Average alcohol by volume is: 3.8 - 5.0%.

Dark Lagers are best when served at 45 - 50 degrees F.

Some ideal food pairings would be hearty and spicy foods, barbecue, sausages and roasted meats. They are also good with Munster cheeses, candied ginger pear cake and pomegranate tarts with walnuts as compliments.

Some of the top selling brands of Dark Lagers in the North America are:

Beck's Dark Lager
Ayinger Altbairisch Dunkel
Kostritzel Schwarzbier
Einbecker Schwarzbier
Speccher Black Bavarian
Warsteiner Dunkel

Lakefront Eastside Dark
Samuel Adams Black Lager
Sapporo Black Lager
Brooklyn Lager
Don Equis XX Amber Lager
Dixie Blackened Voodoo Lager

The ideal glass shapes for Dark & Dunkel Lager are shown on the next page.

Pale Bock, Heller Bock & Maibock

Pale Bock, Heller Bock and Maibock are all part of the Bock family of strong dark lagers. Some of the characteristics of these bock lagers are: an amber colored strong lager with a smooth malty flavor profile and sometimes a hint of hops as well. Bocks are always strong and malty, the darker ones can sometimes be a little sweet.

Average alcohol by volume is 6.5 - 8.0 %.

Pale Bocks, Heller Bocks and Maibock are best when served at: 45 - 50 degrees F.

Some of the ideal food pairings would be spicy foods like Thai or Koren barbecue and even southern fried chicken works well. Swiss cheese, apple almond strudel, white chocolate cheesecake and honey walnut souffle are great compliments to the strong lager.

Some of the top selling brands of Pale Bock, Heller Bock and Maibock in North America are:

Einbecker Mai-Ur Bock   Ayinger Maibock
Hoepfner Maibock   Victory St. Boisterous
Hofbrau Maibock   Gordan Biersch Blonde Bock

The ideal glass shapes for serving Pale Bock, Heller Bock and Maibock are shown on the next page.

Pale Lager (Helles & Dortmunder)

This is a family of beers. Pale Lagers and Standard American Lagers both share a pale color and the traditional lager heritage of the dark lagers, but will differ from dark lagers because of their light color, along with malt and hop balances. Some of the unique characteristics of Pale Lagers are: mildly sweet, light bodied and highly carbonated with low malt and hop presence. They have a nice crisp finish.

Average alcohol by volume is: 4 - 6%.

Pale Lagers are best when served at 40 - 45 degrees F.

Some ideal food pairings would be lighter foods, salads, seafood, pork, chicken and some milder, spicy Asian, Cajun or Latin foods. Some soft and mild cheeses like Wisconsin Butterkase are a great cheese compliment.

Some of the top selling brands of Pale Lagers in North America are:

Pete's Helles Lager	Great Lakes Dortmunder Gold
Augustiner Vollbier Lager	Two Brothers Dog Day Dortmunder Style Lager
Spaten Premium Lager	Firestone Walker Lager
Krampus Imperial Helles Lager	Bell's Lager

The ideal glass shapes for a Pale Lager are shown on the next page.

Classic Premium Pilsners (Lagers)

The original pilsner was first brewed in Pilsen (Pizen), Bohemia in 1842 (now the Czech Republic). The Pilsner Urquell brand defines this style of beer, rarely duplicated and was the first pale lager. Some of the unique characteristics of the Classic Pilsners are: dry, hoppy and light bodied with good hop aromas. They have flavors balanced by fresh malt with a hint of caramel and plenty of aroma and bitterness from the spicy Czech hop called Saaz. The large American breweries have tried to duplicate this style of beer for years.

Average alcohol by volume is: 4.0 - 6.0%.

Classic Pilsners are best when served at 40 - 45 degrees F.

Some ideal food pairings would be lighter foods like chicken, fresh green salads, salmon and milder bratwursts. A mild Vermont white cheddar cheese and light desserts are better compliments.

Some of the top selling brands of Classic Pilsners in North America are:

Pilsner Urquell
Asahi Dry Lager
Brooklyn Pilsner
Czechvar Budvar
FX Matt Accel
Grolsch Premium Pilsner
Schell Pilsner

Summit Pilsner
Live Oaks Pilz
Jever Pils
Harpoon Pilsner
Bitburger Premium Beer
Budweiser Budvar Czech Lager
Victory Prima Pils

The ideal glass shapes for classic pilsner or pils are shown on the next page.

Fruit, Spiced & Smoked Beer

Beyond the classic categories of beer, there are the "special" beers. These are Spiced, Herb or Vegetable Beer, Christmas Specialty Beer, Classic Rauchbier, Smoked Beer, Wood-Aged Beer and Pumpkin Beer. They are all part of the specialty beer family that is pure American ingenuity.

Some of the unique characteristics of Fruit, Spiced & Smoked Beers are: they vary in intensity and strength and are flavored by an assortment of spices, fruits, vegetables, honey and other substances.

Average alcohol by volume is: 2.5 - 12%.

Fruit, Spiced & Smoked Beers are best when served at 50 - 55 degrees F.

The food pairings would be endless, depending on the type of specialty beer you are serving. Try to match up the type of beer with a similar type of food.

Some of the top selling brands of Specialty Beers in North America are:

Leinenkugal's Berry Weiss
Bar Harbour Blueberry Ale
Long Trail Blackberry Wheat
Samuel Adams Cherry Wheat Beer
Buffalo Bills Pumpkin Ale
Harpoon UFO Raspberry Wheat

Pyramid Apricot Weizen
Alaskan Smoked Porter
Pyramid Tilted Kilt Ale
Rogue Smoked Ale
Dogfish Head Midas Touch
Stone's Smoked Porter

The ideal glass shapes for Specialty Beers are shown on the next page, although you can probably serve them in any unusual beer glass.

Kolsch & Altbier Ales

This pair of crisp everyday beer attests to the diversity and ancient brewing traditions in the North of Germany. Both beers are considered specialty beers because they are made using both brewing processes from lagers and ales.

Kolsch is a highly drinkable golden colored ale from the German city of Cologne (Koln) and is a well balanced beer with delicate, clean tasting and rounded flavors. It has soft maltiness and subtle hopping. It is refreshingly light and has a dry hop finish.

Altbier is a dark ale from Dusseldorf and is sometimes called Old Beer. It is a refreshing copper colored beer with clean tasting and fruity undertones, that is a little less malty but with a snappy hop bitterness.

Average alcohol by volume is: 4.3 - 5.3 %.

Kolsch and Altbier Ales are best when served at 40 - 45 degree F.

Some ideal food pairings would be lighter foods, salads, salmon, Monterey Jack cheese, light nutty cheeses, apricot cake or lemon tarts.

Some of the top selling brands of Kolsch & Altbiers ales in North America are:

Goose Island Summertime Kolsch   Leinenkugal Summer Shandy
Long trail Double Bag   Kuppers Kolsch
Reissdorf Kolsch   Zum Uerige Altbier
Southampton Dubuck House Secret Ale Frankenhein Alt
Alaska Summer Ale   New Holland Lucid

The ideal glass shapes for a Kolsch & Altbier Ales are shown on the next page.

Cream Ale & Blonde Ale

Cream and Blonde Ales are hybrid ales from North America that share some of the same characteristics as lagers and ales. Originally a blend of stock pale ale and lager, these ales usually offer more flavor than mass market lagers.

Some of the unique characteristics of Cream and Blonde Ales are: very light bodied, with a touch of sweetness and a hint of hops, light in color.

Average alcohol by volume is: 4.2 - 5.6 %.

Cream and Blonde Ales are best when served at 40 - 45 degrees F .

Some ideal food pairings would be lighter foods, salads, salmon, Monterey Jack cheese, light nutty cheeses, apricot or mandarin orange cake and lemon tarts.

Some of the top selling brands of Cream and Blonde Ales in North America are:

Genesee Cream Ale
Little Kings Cream Ale
Wexford Irish Cream Ale
Anderson Valley Summer Solstice
Red Hook Blonde Ale

New Glarus Spotted Cow
Kiwanda Cream Ale
Rogue Honey Cream Ale
Widmer Blonde Ale

The ideal glass shapes for a Cream and Blonde Ale are shown on the next page.

Steam Beer or California Common Beer

"Steam" is now the trademark of the Anchor Steam Brewing Company in San Francisco, California. It is the last surviving maker of this style of beer that was once extremely popular in western United States. California Common Beer is the generic term for this beer when made by different brewing companies. Steam Beer is the only true indigenous beer made in America.

It is a hybrid beer that is fermented with lager yeast, but at warmer temperatures. It has a rich, light caramely maltiness flavor that is topped off with soft, fruity aromas. It is medium golden in color.

Average alcohol by volume is: 4.0 - 5.4 %.

Steam beer or California Common Beer is best when served at 40 - 45 degrees F.

Some ideal food pairings would be lighter foods, chicken, pork and grilled fish, as well as any light dessert with fresh berries or a light chiffon pie.

The only official brand of Steam Beer sold in the United States is Anchor Steam Beer. Other brands of California Common Beers are:

Flat Earth Element 115
Southampton West Coast Steam Beer

The ideal glass shapes for serving Steam Beer or California Common Beer are shown on the next page.

Tasting Parties
with
Craft Beers

Tasting Parties with Craft Beers

Beer Tastings are for a special occasion when you want your guests to sample a variety of different beers from various breweries. Today, craft beers are available at almost any high end grocery or liquor store. More and more retailers are carrying a larger variety of craft beers from all over the world. In the United States, it is the fastest growing adult beverage category. You'll need several different craft beers. I suggest several different light pilsners and darker beers like porters and stouts. Always start your beer tastings evening with lighter beers and end with darker beers.

A simple golden rule about serving craft beers: lighter beers are normally served cold and darker beers are served slightly chilled or at room temperature. But be sure to look at the carton or bottle, as some newer craft beers have different guide lines.

Many different beer glasses and mugs are available to help you experience the fullest tasting experience possible. I've used several different mini beer tasters because they are small enough to give each guest a small taste of each of these craft beers. Narrower glasses are best for lighter pilsners and wider glasses are best for darker craft beers.

Be sure to serve your favorite craft brews with some delicious tasting appetizers. There are many books available that explain the right food to serve with your favorite craft or specialty brews. I've listed a few for each of the different styles of craft beer.

Having a craft beer tasting party is a great way to bring friends and family together for something a little different and a unique way to try many different types of craft beer from all over the world, especially when served with multiple tasting appetizers.

Many chefs today believe beer is a better compliment with food than wine. Some agree or disagree for many reasons. But one thing is for certain, it is much more affordable to experiment with beer and food pairing than with wine.

Tasting parties can be as simple or as elaborate as you want them to be. You'll be surprised that even during a special event like a Super Bowl Party, having a variety of craft beers helps make the celebration that much more special and festive. Above I've used a mini pilsner and a mini mug for a simple tasting party.

Another example of a little more elaborate Beer Tasting Party idea would be to use several different beer tasting glasses and compliment these craft beers with some light appetizers. There are many different tasting party products in the marketplace that will help you with this tasting party presentation. Small glass and ceramic dishes are great for serving those small bite size portions of your favorite appetizer or dessert to compliment your favorite craft beer.

Another great Tasting Parties idea or presentation when entertaining would be to use several different craft beers along with several different mini-cocktails recipes and a bottle or two of your favorite red and white wine. Again, I always compliment the alcoholic beverages with some simple, yet delicious, appetizers and desserts. You should always serve some sort of food when you are serving alcohol. Something as simple as a bag of pretzels will work, but I'd suggest some simple appetizers to compliment your craft beers. That is what a tasting part is all about.

Cocktails made with Craft Beer

Beer Margarita

Take an American classic, the Mexican Margarita, mix it with a wonderful craft beer and you have a true new American Classic, a Beer Margarita. Serve it in a traditional margarita stem or a clunky double old fashion. Either way, it will look and taste great.

Here is what you will need to make 4 servings in a glass pitcher.

2 - 12oz bottles of beer
1/2 cup frozen concentrate limeade, thawed
1/2 cup chilled tequila
1 lime, cut into pieces
1/4 cup coarse sea salt or margarita salt
crushed ice cubes (about 16-20)

Rub the lime wedges around the rim of the glass and then dip the rim into a saucer of salt.

In a medium glass pitcher, combine the beer, tequila and limeade. Stir until mixed well. Serve in the glasses and garnish with a lime wedge. Enjoy !

Beer Party Punch

This is a new twist to the ordinary party punch. It's cool and refreshing and I think the guys will love it too. Beer Party Punch will add a lot of pizzazz to any party and is great for when you need to serve a lot of people at one time.

Here is what you will need to make a container full of Beer Party Punch.

1 cup fresh or frozen raspberries or blackberries or both
4 - 12oz bottles of chilled beer, like a pilsner
12 oz frozen raspberry lemonade from concentrate; add water from can
1/2 cup vodka
2 lemons and 2 limes, sliced

In a large container, pitcher or punch bowl, mix together the first four ingredients until the frozen concentrate is completely dissolved. Add a few lemon and lime slices to the container. Use the remaining lemon and lime slices for garnishes for each of the serving glasses. Enjoy !

Spiked Apple Ale Cocktail

Some of the trendy bars in New York City are offering many new and exciting cocktails made with beer and spirits. This one will be sure to grab your attention. It is called a Spiked Apple because you use Apple Liqueur. You can make an Orange Spiked Lager using orange liqueur or a Peach Spiked Brew using peach schnapps.

This recipe makes 2-3 cocktails. You will need one small glass pitcher.

2 - 12 oz bottle of any lager beer, chilled
4 oz apple liqueur or orange liqueur or peach liqueur
a few ice cubes

Mix everything together in a glass pitcher. Pour into individual cocktail or beer glasses. Serve and Enjoy !

Traditional Boilermaker

Nothing is more ordinary or everyday but fun and crazy as an Boilermaker. Who likes them, I'm not sure, but here is the simple recipe that will help start the party.

This will make one boilermaker in a very sleek beer glass.

1 - 12 oz craft beer
2 oz whiskey

You can make this two different ways. Pour a bottle of beer into a beer glass and add the shot of whiskey or serve the glass of beer with a shot glass of whiskey on the side. Either way, it's a traditional boilermaker. Enjoy !

Beer Martini

This is another one of the classic cocktails with a unique twist. I always try to use a very good gin and a high quality beer. You and your guests will appreciate it in the end.

This will make enough for 4-5 martinis. You'll need a small glass pitcher to mix the martinis in and several martini glasses for serving.

8 oz pale ale, cold
12 oz gin, chilled to very cold
several ice cubes

12 olives, garlic stuffed are perfect, but blue cheese olives work great as well
4-5 toothpicks

Put the first three ingredients in the glass pitcher or cocktail shaker and stir. Strain and pour into the chilled martini glasses. Place three olives on each toothpick and put into each glass. Enjoy !

Beer Sangria

Wow ! This is an incredible party cocktail that your guests will just love. I like to serve it when I'm grilling some brats or making a mixed grill of brats, pork chops and chicken. Add a tossed salad and you are ready to go. This will make enough for 4-6 servings in a 12 oz beer glass.

You will need a large glass pitcher and several cool beer or cocktail glasses.

4 - 12 oz bottles of a good lager, chilled
1 cup triple sec
1 cup fresh lemon juice
1 cup canned pears, mashed or pureed
2 fresh pears, sliced. Use 1 sliced pear in the pitcher and one for garnishing (optional)
several ice cubes per glass

In the pitcher, add the first five ingredients and mix well. Add some ice and you are ready to go. Garnish with a pear slice. Enjoy !

Mexican Michelada

This is a true Mexican cocktail. Some will make it without the tequila, but a true Mexican Michelada cocktail will always have the tequila. My friends in Monterrey, Mexico have told me it will knock your socks off and I really cannot disagree with them.

You'll need a large glass pitcher and several beer glasses for serving.

4 - 12 oz bottles of cold craft beer
juice from 4 small lemons or 6-8 oz lemon juice
8 oz tequila
dash of soy sauce
dash of Tabasco Sauce
dash of Worcestershire Sauce
pinch of salt & pepper
2 cups ice cubes

In the glass pitcher, add about 2 cups of ice cubes. Add the craft beer, tequila and lemon juice. Stir. Add the soy sauce, Tabasco Sauce and Worcestershire Sauce and salt and pepper. Stir and Serve. These are especially good when served with tamales. Enjoy !

Classic Shandy Gaff

This is a 17th century Old English tradition. Some say it was named after a local English pub that served less than quality beer and flavored it with sweet lemonade. Tradition or no tradition, it is a very refreshing, tangy, tasty beer cocktail.

This recipe will make one cocktail in a tall 16 oz pilsner style glass.

1 - 12 oz bottle of American Pale Ale, chilled
4 oz spicy ginger beer or ginger ale or lemonade or even limeade
a few ice cubes, optional
several lemon wedges for garnish

Pour the lager beer into the tall pilsner glass and top it off with the ginger beer. Add a couple of ice cubes if desired. Serve and Enjoy !

Crazy Snakebite

This is another one of those beer combinations that will please just about anyone. Again, it's a pretty simple cocktail to make but bursting with a unique flavor. This is a great beer cocktail for the fall or autumn of the year, right when the leaves are turning those beautiful fall colors. Sit back and enjoy both of them together while watching a football game.

This recipe will make two Snakebite cocktails. You will need two very cool beer glasses.

1 -12 oz bottle of a lager beer
12 oz of apple cider

Pour 6 oz of beer into each beer glass. Top off each glass with 6oz of apple cider. Stir and Serve. Enjoy !

Mary Red Eye

Nothing is as simple as this little puppy, a classic Bloody Mary made with beer. I serve it in a tall pilsner glass to make it a little more exotic, yet really refreshing.

The recipe will make a small pitcher full. You will need a small glass pitcher and several tall pilsner glasses for serving.

1 - 12 oz bottle of beer
1 large can of tomato or V-8 juice
splash of Tabasco Sauce
dash of Worcestershire Sauce
some ice cubes

several stalks of celery for garnish

Pour the first two ingredients into the pitcher and stir. Add the Tabasco and Worcestershire sauce a little at a time to suit your taste. Add a few ice cubes if desired. Garnish with a celery stick in each glass. That simple, that quick. Serve and Enjoy !

Bee Sting

This is another beer cocktail that sounds familiar but is very different from the original screwdriver most of us grew up with. It has a little more zest or zing than normal, but what's normal anyways? You'll love it.

This recipe will make a small pitcher full of cocktails. You will need a small glass pitcher and several beer pilsners or tall skinny glasses for serving.

2 - 12 oz bottles of any dark craft beer, chilled
3 cups or 24 oz orange juice, chilled
a few orange slices for garnish (optional)

Pour both the beer and orange juice into the pitcher and stir. You are ready to go. Garnish each glass with a orange slice. Serve and Enjoy !

Skip & Go Naked

An associate of mine brought this killer beer cocktail to my attention from her younger days of enjoying a fun filled evening with friends. The name might be strange, but it has been said to be quite the kick in the butt cocktail.

Take a large glass pitcher and fill it with one can of frozen limeade, one can of vodka and 2 bottles of any light beer. Stir. Garnish each glass with a lime wedge. I sometimes put everything in a blender for a frothy, frozen cocktail. Either way, they are powerful and refreshing. Enjoy !

Caribbean Night Cap

This is one of those night caps that won't put you to sleep right away. But who wants to go to bed so early anyway, especially when you are relaxing at night by the pool or on the beach in St. Thomas?

This recipe will make two glasses of a Caribbean Night Cap for you and a good friend or companion. You will need two short beer glasses for serving.

One 12 oz bottle of Chocolate Stout
2 ounces coffee liqueur

Start with two footed pilsner glasses. Pour half of the chocolate stout in each glass. Add 1 ounce of coffee liqueur to each glass and mix together. Enjoy !

Mix everything together in the glass pitcher and stir. Serve and Enjoy !

Caffeine Bomber

What a quick pick me up and pick you up it will. This is not for the faint of heart. It is a new high-powered energizer drink. It's a great cocktail right before you want to go out on a night on the town or be up all night watching scary movies.

This recipe will make enough for two good size cocktails. You will need a small glass pitcher for serving and two very sexy beer glasses.

1 - 12 oz bottle of Newcastle Brown Ale, chilled
1 shot of espresso
1 shot of Jack Daniels
1 can of Red Bull

Mix everything together in the glass pitcher and stir. Serve and Enjoy !

Broadway Diesel

This magnificent cocktail got its start in Japan or is at least very popular in Japan as tradition goes. An associate of mine has family in Japan and they enjoy these during their more popular holidays.

This recipe will make enough for two cocktails. You will need two very special beer pilsners.

1 - 12 oz bottle of any lager beer
1 - 12 oz can of any cola

Pour the beer equally into the two beer pilsners. Top off equally with the cola in each glass. You don't need to be a rocket scientist to make this wonderful and refreshing cocktail. Just mix it up and serve. Enjoy !

Beth's Black Raspberry

This cocktail is light, refreshing and a little on the sweet side. Beth will always add some extra stout to make it a little more tart. This recipe will make 2-3 flavored cocktails.

one bottle of any Lambic or Framboise craft beer
one bottle of any Dark Stout, Chocolate Stout or Imperial Stout

Fill a beautiful, slender beer pilsner with any fruity Lambic or Framboise to about 3/4 full and top off with any type of your favorite stout. Stir slightly and serve. Enjoy !

Blow My Skull Off

They don't get any more powerful than this little cocktail! Not for the light of heart or somebody who wants a sissy drink. This one is a killer cocktail but a quite tasty one at that. If you like spicy food, you'll love this cocktail.

This will make enough for two cocktails. You will need two beer pilsners or any sleek cool cocktail glasses.

1 - 12 oz bottle of stout or dark beer
4 oz dark rum or Captain Morgan's Spiced Rum
4 oz lime juice
pinch of cayenne pepper
2 lime slices or wedges for garnish

Pour half or 6 oz of the stout in each beer glass. Then add 2 oz of rum and lime juice to each glass. Mix well. Add a pinch of cayenne pepper to each glass, more or less depending on how spicy you want it to be. Stir slightly. Garnish with a lime wedge. Serve and Enjoy !

INDEX

About the author.

This is ROBERT ZOLLWEG's seventh book. This one on **Craft Brews** is a little different from his first six books. His first three were cookbooks, one on **Just Mini Desserts**, the second on **Just Tastings** with mini appetizers, soups and salads and his third one was on **Just Mini Cocktails**, which continued this passion for entertaining with the tasting party theme. His fourth and fifth were on **Just Home Decor** and **Creative Accents**, decorating tips with glass centerpieces for your home. The sixth was on **Just Baking**. He is a native of Toledo, Ohio and has been in the tabletop industry for almost 40 years. He designs glassware, flatware and ceramic products for the retail and foodservice industry. He has worked with all of the major retailers including Crate and Barrel, Macy's, Pier One Imports, Cost Plus World Market, Bed Bath & Beyond, JCPenneys, Target, Kohl's, Walmart, Sears and Home Outfitters to name a few. Most of his professional career has been with Libbey Glass in Toledo, Ohio. He has traveled the world extensively looking for color and design trends and the right products to design and bring to the retail and foodservice marketplace.

Robert has always had a passion for entertaining. He is also an artist-painter and works primarily with acrylic on canvas using bold primary colors. He currently lives in his home in Toledo's Historic Old West End and in the artistic community of Saugatuck, Michigan.

To find more information about Robert Zollweg, visit his web site at: www.zollwegart.com

Just mini Cocktails

cocktails & party drinks

Fun & Exciting Cocktail Recipes
for casual entertaining
and tasting parties
by Robert Zollweg

Creative accents
home décor ideas with glass

Decorative Home

Wedding & Bridal

Holiday Centerpieces

Young & Modern

Craft Ideas

Fun & Exciting Home Décor
decorating ideas with
glass centerpieces
by Robert Zollweg

HOME décor
creative ideas with glass

Decorative Accessories
Wedding & Bridal
Holiday Centerpieces
Young & Modern
Craft Ideas
Bed & Bath

Fun & Exciting Home Décor
decorating ideas with
glass centerpieces
by Robert Zollweg

Just Tasting

mini appetizers
soups & salads

Quick and Easy Recipes
mini appetizers soups & salads
by Robert Zollweg   for casual entertaining

CRAFT BREWS
the right glass for the right beer

ales and lagers
beer cocktails
food pairing with craft beers
by Robert Zollweg

Just Baking
mini pies and casseroles

Quick and Easy
Single Serving Recipes
by Robert Zollweg   for casual family entertaining

Just Mini Desserts

Quick and Easy
Mini Dessert Recipes
for Casual Entertaining
by Robert Zollweg

I hope you have enjoyed my book on **Craft Brews**. It should help you understand more about serving the right beer in the right glass and to make your next casual get together or tasting party a lot more fun and exciting.

Any of my cookbooks or home décor books would be a wonderful compliment to anyone's home entertaining cookbook collection. They are all available at area retailers or on my web site at:
www.zollwegart.com

Enjoy !   Robert

127